Would You I for Kids

Over 100+ of Hilarious, Challenging & Silly Questions for The Entire Family to Enjoy Hours of Fun

FunnyLuck Publishing

Copyright © 2019 by FunnyLuck Publishing

All rights reserved. This book or any portion there of may not be reproduced or used in any manner whatsoever without the express written permission of the publisher except for the use of brief quotations in a book review.

ISBN 9781086427622

Introduction

Would you rather questions are a great way to get a conversation started in a fun and interesting way. And it's easy to get into some amazing conversations by just asking "why" after a would you rather question. You'll get some very interesting answers and probably learn a lot more about the person you are talking to. It is fun and anyone can play this game especially with your family.

How to Play?

1. Play with at least two players

2. Choose a player to go first- Select the first player, who will choose a question that begins with "Would you rather...?" and provides two scenarios from this book for another player to choose from

3. Choose one answer to any question you are asked

4. Continue asking and answering questions until there isn't any left.

Bonus Variation

❖ Play in a group

❖ Set a time limit- to help speed up the game and encourage split-second decisions.

Would You Rather

be in an animation movie

 **OR**

in an action movie

eat your favorite meal

 **OR**

eat a meal you've never had before?

Would You Rather

be popular among your classmates

 **OR**

be popular among your teachers?

in a house filled with marshmallows

 **OR**

a house filled with candy?

Would You Rather

be able to make plants grow very quickly

 OR

be able to make it rain whenever you wanted?

have bright pink hair

 OR

bright brown hair?

Would You Rather

it was winter all the time

 **OR**

that it was summer all the time?

wear trendy sneakers

 **OR**

wear cute shoes?

Would You Rather

rather clean up your bathroom

 **OR**

clean up your bedroom?

get a huge bowl of punch

 **OR**

or get a huge bowl of ice-cream?

Would You Rather

have 100$ now

 **OR**

1000$ in a year?

get a toy boat

 **OR**

go see a real-life ship?

Would You Rather

have your friends come over

 **OR**

go outside and play with your friends?

go for a stroll

 **OR**

drive around with dad in his car?

Would You Rather

have only white clothes

only multicolored clothes?

own a restaurant

be a chef?

Would You Rather

have your mom stay at home all day

 **OR**

go with mom to work?

walk around with soap in your hair

 **OR**

with an unkempt hair?

Would You Rather

have pizza

 **OR**

have a hotdog?

eat your chips with ketchup

 **OR**

eat your chips with mustard?

Would You Rather

go to school with your friend on the public bus

 **OR**

with mom and dad?

do hand-painting

 **OR**

paint with a brush?

Would You Rather

go swimming

 **OR**

relax beside the pool?

be able to change colors like a chameleon

 **OR**

hold your breath underwater for an hour?

Would You Rather

be lost in the woods at night

 **OR**

stuck in a haunted house at night?

drive a racecar

 **OR**

pilot an airplane?

Would You Rather

play in the snow

 **OR**

at the beach?

Live in a giant peach

 **OR**

Live in a giant shoe?

Would You Rather

drop your new phone down to the toilet

 **OR**

drop your charm bracelet down the sink?

do a marathon of Disney movies of your choosing

 **OR**

Pixar movies of your choosing?

Would You Rather

do your homework

 **OR**

finish a whole bottle of plain milk?

be surprised by a present

 **OR**

be able to pick what you get?

Would You Rather

be a Unicorn

 OR

be a Wizard?

wake up early

 OR

eat raw spinach in breakfast?

Would You Rather

be a firefighter

 **OR**

a police officer?

hang out for an hour with 10 puppies

 **OR**

10 kittens?

Would You Rather

be super strong

 **OR**

super fast?

have a robot to be your friend

 **OR**

do your chores?

Would You Rather

live in the Star Trek universe

 OR

the Star Wars universe?

discover dinosaur fossils

 OR

a meteorite in your back yard?

Would You Rather

have the ability to fly

 **OR**

to be invisible?

pet a giraffe

 **OR**

pet a hippopotamus?

Would You Rather

watch people ice-skate

 OR

go ice-skating?

cuddle a big teddy

 OR

cuddle with mom?

Would You Rather

meet a fairy

 **OR**

meet a goddess?

go to a birthday party

 **OR**

plan a birthday party?

Would You Rather

have a big room

 OR

a big backyard?

live with grandma

 OR

live with your cousins?

Would You Rather

go to a boarding school

 OR

go to a day school?

be homeschooled

 OR

go to a regular school?

Would You Rather

be in a dance class

 OR

be in the choir?

shower with cold water

 OR

with hot water?

Would You Rather

lose your favorite blanket

 **OR**

your favorite Teddy bear?

watch cartoons

 **OR**

dress up as cartoon characters?

Would You Rather

rather listen to an audiobook

 **OR**

read a hardcover book?

find a pony on your own

be surprised with a pony?

Would You Rather

have all the drinks you could ever want

 **OR**

all the junk food you could ever want?

go to summer school

 **OR**

summer camp?

Would You Rather

go to a tea party

 **OR**

a costume party?

have a very powerful telescope

 **OR**

a very powerful microscope?

Would You Rather

play on the slides

 **OR**

on the trampoline?

get good grades

 **OR**

be really good at a sport?

Would You Rather

help set the table for dinner

 **OR**

help clear the table after dinner?

eat candy for the rest of your life

 **OR**

never eat candy again?

Would You Rather

go to the moon

 **OR**

go to the bottom of the ocean?

rather build a snowman

 **OR**

build a sand castle?

Would You Rather

be Spiderman's sidekick

Superman's sidekick?

rather crawl around all the time

hop around all the time?

Would You Rather

drink hot chocolate

 **OR**

chocolate milk?

meet a friendly dinosaur

 **OR**

meet a friendly dragon?

Would You Rather

keep your money with Dad

 **OR**

Mom?

be in a food fight

 **OR**

just watch a food fight?

Would You Rather

be able to spit out ice

 OR

spit out fire?

be able to talk to animals

 OR

be able to hear animals talk?

Would You Rather

wake up with wings

 OR

wake up with a tail?

get a brain freeze every time you drank something cold

 OR

stop drinking anything cold altogether?

Would You Rather

meet someone who has four eyes

 **OR**

someone with three mouths?

be in your favorite video game

 **OR**

be in your favorite cartoon?

Would You Rather

make loud burps that are hard to ignore

 **OR**

burps that smell really bad?

have a rabbit's ears

 **OR**

a rabbit's teeth?

Would You Rather

not have toilet paper while you're on the toilet seat

 **OR**

not have water to wash your hands with afterward?

be in your favorite video game

 **OR**

be in your favorite cartoon?

Would You Rather

meet a donkey that walks on two legs

 **OR**

a donkey that talks?

poop chocolate

 **OR**

have poop that smells like Strawberry?

Would You Rather

have no eyebrows

 OR

have green eyebrows?

have milk run down your nose every time you laugh

 OR

have milk run out of your eyes every time you cried?

Would You Rather

have your leg stuck in the toilet bowl

 **OR**

have your hands stuck in the toilet bowl?

lick milk like a cat

 **OR**

lick yourself like a cat?

Would You Rather

dance around the house in your funny costume

 OR

dance around the neighborhood barefooted?

be without a nose

 OR

be without ears?

Would You Rather

have to poop every hour

 **OR**

have to pee every hour?

not be able to taste anything

 **OR**

not be able to smell anything?

Would You Rather

have seven fingers

 **OR**

have seven toes?

have gum stuck to the bottom of your shoe

 **OR**

plastic paper stuck to the bottom of your shoe?

Would You Rather

touch your own poop

 **OR**

dog poop?

have a stain on your outfit and not notice

 **OR**

a hole in your outfit and not notice?

Would You Rather

be pranked by covering in slime

 **OR**

be a well-known prankster?

meet a kind monster

 **OR**

a monster who's looking for friends?

Would You Rather

be bald

 **OR**

have hair that's almost touching the floor?

have all your teeth fall out

 **OR**

have only two teeth?

Would You Rather

be stuck in school for 6 months

 **OR**

get assignments every single day for 6 months?

brush your teeth with mustard

 **OR**

brush your teeth with chilli sauce?

Would You Rather

have a really scary smile

 **OR**

have a really loud laugh?

to read the minds of babies

 **OR**

be able to communicate with babies?

Would You Rather

eat a year's worth of burger in one night

 OR

never eat burgers again?

have embarrassing pictures of you posted online

 OR

sent to your crush?

Would You Rather

dance like a chicken in front of your friends

 **OR**

dance like a chicken on the internet?

be stuck in a toilet because your poop won't flush

 **OR**

because the toilet door won't open?

Would You Rather

have a squeaky voice

a really loud voice?

get into a fight with chickens

get chased by chickens?

Would You Rather

have a toy that walks

 **OR**

a toy that talks?

find a lizard hiding in your pizza

 **OR**

cockroach hiding in your shoe?

Would You Rather

tame a dinosaur

 **OR**

tame a gorilla?

be pranked with a fake rat

 **OR**

a fake bug?

Would You Rather

pee in a bucket

 **OR**

pee in a cup?

have a bird make a nest in your hair

 **OR**

a chicken lay eggs in your hair?

Would You Rather

have blue skin like an alien

really white skin?

have multicolored hair

hair that tastes like candy?

Would You Rather

live in the sky permanently

live underwater permanently?

have a bird make a nest in your hair

a chicken lay eggs in your hair?

Would You Rather

be able to turn yourself into a butterfly

 **OR**

be able to turn yourself into an eagle?

be able to climb walls like a spider

 **OR**

run as fast as a rodent?

Would You Rather

live in the sky permanently

live underwater permanently?

have a bird make a nest in your hair

a chicken lay eggs in your hair?

Would You Rather

be able to talk to animals

 **OR**

be able to be an animal of your choice?

look really old

 **OR**

look like a newborn baby again?

Would You Rather

eat a piece of gum from the street

 OR

give your already chewed gum to someone else?

sleep beside a panda

 OR

sleep beside a cow?

Would You Rather

eat only donuts for an entire week

 **OR**

never get to eat donuts for the rest of your life?

look really old

 **OR**

have an itch that refuses to go away?

Would You Rather

dip your face into a plate of sauce

 **OR**

into a plate of blended garlic?

live in a world full of zombies

 **OR**

a world full of aliens?

Would You Rather

rather go to a dance with someone who has bad skill

 **OR**

someone who has body odor?

have your mom embarrass you at school

 **OR**

have your friend embarrass you at school?

Would You Rather

poop in your pants when scared

 **OR**

pee on yourself when scared?

be the star player on a losing sports team at school

 **OR**

ride the bench on a sports team that always wins?

Would You Rather

sing with a crooked voice in front of your schoolmates

 **OR**

sing in a crooked voice in front of a stranger?

your underwear's were all pink

 **OR**

all your underwear's had holes in them?

Would You Rather

wake up with your grandma's face

 **OR**

wake up with your grandpa's face?

have nosy friends

 **OR**

noisy friends?

Would You Rather

be very unpopular

 **OR**

be super popular in school?

only be able to listen to music from the 70's

 **OR**

never be able to listen to music again?

Would You Rather

be stuck on an island alone

 **OR**

be stuck with someone who won't stop screaming?

in a cave alone

 **OR**

live in a cave with a friendly bear?

Would You Rather

with a crying baby for a day

 **OR**

with a baby that likes to drag your hair?

have really large feet

 **OR**

feet so small you have to wear a baby shoes

Would You Rather

kiss your Teddy bear before sleeping

 **OR**

whisper to it all through the night?

sleep alone when it's raining heavily

 **OR**

creep into your sibling's room and sleep together?

Would You Rather

run from a rabbit that talks

 **OR**

a rabbit that walks on two feet?

have hair grow on your tongue

 **OR**

have hair grow in between your teeth?

Would You Rather

throw up on your crush

 **OR**

throw up on your best friend?

sing loudly in the shower

 **OR**

sing loudly while on the toilet seat?

Would You Rather

never have to take another test in school

 **OR**

never get sick ever again?

get to skip whatever class you wanted every single day

 **OR**

get however much screen time you wanted

Would You Rather

get to eat whatever you want, whenever you want,

 **OR**

get to go to bed whenever you want?

have an actual robot dog

 **OR**

an actual rocket?

Would You Rather

be able to go back in time

 **OR**

have the power to stop time whenever you want?

rather live forever

 **OR**

never feel pain?

Would You Rather

rather fart in an elevator on your way to class

 **OR**

fart in class?

wear pajamas to class

 **OR**

go to class in your underwear?

Would You Rather

do a prank phone call

 **OR**

send a prank text?

show up to school on the back of a dinosaur

 **OR**

eat food straight from the pot?

Would You Rather

swim in ice-cold water

 **OR**

swim in a pool of hot water?

eat an entire cake on your own

 **OR**

eat 12 boxes of pizza on your own?

Would You Rather

be an engineer

 **OR**

a famous actor when you grow up?

win an Olympic gold medal

 **OR**

win a million dollar in the lottery?

Would You Rather

roll down the stairs

hop down the stairs?

have food spilled all over your favorite outfit

have a drink spilled all over your favorite outfit?

Would You Rather

ride on the back of a lion

 **OR**

ride on the back of a tiger?

have an aunt that pulls your cheeks a lot

 **OR**

an aunt that pats your head a lot?

Would You Rather

forget to take your toothbrush for a sleepover

 OR

forget to take your towel for a sleepover?

scream while watching a scary movie

 OR

pee in your pants while watching a scary movie?

Would You Rather

have a nose as long as Pinocchio's

 OR

no nose at all?

be elected class president

 OR

nominated homecoming king / queen?

Would You Rather

forget the way to school

 **OR**

forget the way to your class?

have your diary read out in public

 **OR**

eaten by your dog?

Would You Rather

rather have the entire school know who you're crushing on OR

never get to see your crush again?

ride on the back of an elephant OR

a hippo?

Would You Rather

fall asleep in class

 OR

fall asleep on the bus?

eat food out of the trashcan

 OR

not get any food to eat for an entire weekend?

Would You Rather

live in a house made of gummy bears

 **OR**

marshmallows?

have a nightmare again

 **OR**

never get the flu every again?

Would You Rather

eat liver

 **OR**

sardines for dinner for the rest of your life?

be the best singer

 **OR**

the best dancer in your entire school?

Would You Rather

be respected by all of your peers

 **OR**

feared by them?

be captain of the basketball team

 **OR**

captain of the debate team?

Would You Rather

be great at math

 **OR**

great at English?

ace every single test you took without studying

 **OR**

win every single sports game you played?

Just One More Favor I Need From You...

Hope you have enjoyed and had a great time playing this game!

Reviews are one of the most important factors in a book's success. Even if you are a bestselling author, your new book--which you have toiled on for years--can have its chances of success ruined within a matter of moments by a few negative reviews (genuine or not).

It would mean so much to me if you would take a moment to visit the page (or any of my other titles) and leave an honest review, whether positive or negative.

To vote or review, just click on the link below.

Made in the USA
San Bernardino, CA
10 November 2019

59708557R00058